About WAY OF THE

Join best-selling author and police officer Bernard Schaffer as he examines the philosophy of modern Law Enforcement. A sixteen year veteran and second-generation cop, Schaffer possesses a keen insight into what it takes to successfully uphold the law and not lose your mind in the process.

Equal parts biography and instructional guide, Way of the Warrior focuses on the core of the individual officer: the warrior spirit.

Whether you're a grunt working The Street or a white shirt who'd need a GPS to find it, this guide is designed to help you reconnect with why you took the oath to serve and protect. Behind the badge and the gun lies the heart of a warrior. Unleash your inner hero.

WAY of the WARRIOR

Law Enforcement Philosophy by Bernard Schaffer

CONTENTS

1. Blue Beginnings
2. Stark Realities
3. Training and Equipment
4. The True Blue Line
5. Schaffer's Eight Golden Rules of Criminal Investigation
6. The Unsolvable Problem of Police Work (A Starter's Guide)
7. Back to the Start
8. A Word about this Edition

About the Author

Copyright

1. Blue Beginnings

As a boy, I dreamt of belonging to a warrior society.

I was fascinated by knights, samurai, musketeers, Vikings, and Spartans. I spent long hours in the fields surrounding our family home with battery- operated toy machine guns and large plastic knives, playing war games. Later, when I was old enough to own a bb gun, I hunted small game like field mice with the fervor of a young Davey Crockett.

On the day I turned twelve years old, my father proudly informed me that it was time to attend "Hunter Safety Class."

Graduates of the safety class are presented with orange cards that officially license them as hunters in the Commonwealth of Pennsylvania. It was permission to carry a gun and shoot things. My father had hunted since he was a little boy. My uncles hunted. Even my older cousin Kimberly hunted. She pulled her long ponytail through the back of her orange baseball cap to keep it out of the way when she shot.

The beginning of deer season was always a big event in our house. My dad would leave before the crack of dawn on the first day of deer season and we wouldn't see him again for several days. He'd come home with a scruffy beard, stinking of earth and game, but more times than not he was carrying freezer bags full of fresh meat.

My mother is Italian, and the only way she could tolerate venison was by using it as an ingredient with her regular dishes. She was used to making heaping bowls of ravioli and sausage spicy enough to make your eyes water, all of it covered with enough red gravy to drown a family of turtles. She detested deer meat, but she'd still cook up whatever my old man dragged home. To this day, if I eat venison, it's probably been turned into a meatball.

Voyages into the great outdoors with my father were always fraught with disaster. As a little kid he'd take me fishing with two pairs of clothes because invariably, I would fall in the water. We once went on a fishing trip with the guys from his police department for bluefish, my first time on a boat, and I spent the whole time bent over the side, chumming in my own special way.

As an outdoorsman, I was better by myself. I liked to go out into the woods with my pocket knife and whittle sticks, or practice walking through thick brush making as little noise as possible. It was always some kind of game. It was never just me practicing sneaking around in the woods. I was Sitting Bull, looking for a whiteman to scalp. It was never me putting a bb into the rear end of a squirrel. I was a safari hunter, taking out a predator.

Once I got my license, our first actual hunts were made in the large corn fields across from my house, searching for pheasant. Back in those days, the undeveloped areas of Montgomery County were a haven for pheasant. You'd go outside for a walk and kick up at least a half dozen of them, easily.

Today, they're all gone.

The combination of urban sprawl, pesticides, loss of wetlands, and increased farming practices, means there simply isn't much room for them anymore. If someone says they're going to hunt pheasant nowadays, it means they are going to a wildlife preserve out in New Jersey.

But back then, all you needed was an orange vest, a shotgun, and a good dog. Our springer spaniel would flush out birds all day and night. She'd stand there at the door when I was watching television, just staring at them in the fields, thinking, "Soon. Very, very soon."

My old man was a terrible hunting partner. The second the dog kicked one up, he'd shoot it. He'd stand there looking at me over the smoking barrel of his gun and say, "Why didn't you fire, slow poke?"

We cleaned the birds in the basement and I'd watch him pluck all the feathers off and start cutting them apart with his pocket knife. He'd make me hold various organs and say, "Do you know what that is?"

Nope. I just know I don't feel very hungry anymore.

"You better get hungry," he said. "It's a damn sin to shoot anything you don't intend on eating. We shot that bird, and we're gonna eat it."

After that, the field mice and squirrels around my house were pretty much given a permanent stay of execution. The only things I shot with my bb gun were empty beer cans, and if one thing is for certain, with my dad, there are always plenty of them around.

Still, it seemed a very primal thing to feed one's family with something you'd harvested from the Great Outdoors. The hunters return to provide for the gatherers. The men, along with my cousin Kimberly, would drag the bloody beef back into the caves for the women to cook. It connected me to my ancient ancestors. It was how I would become a man.

Unfortunately, becoming a man means getting up really, really early in the morning and freezing your ass off.

We were in Tinicum Township in Bucks County at my Uncle Jimmy and Aunt Kathy's place, and it was pitch black when the alarm went off. I think if you'd offered me a strange blood-letting rite or body scarification ritual in exchange for a few extra hours of sleep, I'd have taken you up on the offer.

That morning, my aunt cooked breakfast for all of us and even passed me one of the cups of coffee. I told her I didn't know if I was allowed to have any and she patted me on the head and said, "You're going to need it. It's cold as heck out there."

My Dad and I got dressed in long-johns and flannel shirts. We put on heavy coats and orange safety vests and hats and marched out into the cold woods. He told me to move quietly and look for signs of deer. "What kind of signs?" I said.

He pointed at a small clump of black pellets that looked like raisins and said, "Like that. Is it fresh?"

I looked at the deer shit and said, "Exactly how am I supposed to know that?"

He rolled his eyes and bent over and picked up a few of the pellets and said, "No, it's old. Keep moving."

We made our way into a tree stand and I sat there with my twelve-gauge pump at the ready. At the ready. At the…"Dad, where are all the deer?"

"Nowhere if you don't stop talking," he whispered.

"We see deer all the time back home. You can't drive down the road and not see twenty of them. Maybe we need to get in our car and go look for them."

"Would you shut up before I throw you out of the tree stand? Your cousin Kimberly complains less than this, you big sissy."

After that, I sat there as quiet as I could, holding my gun, trying not to freeze to death. My Uncle Jimmy was somewhere else in the woods, trying to push the deer into the open. Eventually, my dad's walkie-talkie crackled, and Jimmy said, "Couple headed your way, Bern. I saw a big buck and a few doe."

The excitement in my dad's voice was palpable when he put down the walkie-talkie and told me, "Get ready, buddy. Here they come."

After all that sitting and all that waiting, it was now time to go. Suddenly, three deer crashed through the brush, running and jumping so fast I couldn't tell which one had antlers. My Dad shouted, "Shoot it! Shoot it!"

I raised my gun and aimed at the biggest animal, hoping it was the right thing to shoot. My hands were surprisingly steady as I centered the shotgun's site on the buck's chest and squeezed the trigger. The stock recoiled into my shoulder and the deer folded in half like it had been punched in the stomach. Then, to my utter disbelief, it got up and kept running.

"Gutshot!" my Dad hollered. "Shoot it again!"

I fumbled when I tried to rack the slide but couldn't get it to work right. I wound up stove-piping the spent shell casing in the ejection port and the gun jammed. The deer was long gone by the time I finally got another one in the chamber.

You'd have thought I dropped the winning touchdown at the Superbowl.

The old man hooted and hollered from the time he said, "Shoot it again!" until we got down from the tree stand. We found the blood trail and tracked that damn deer for hours, but it was useless. My first deer, the symbolic kill that was to complete my journey into manhood, was a complete bust.

My father's disappointment was monumental. He still talks about it. I remember firing that shot like it was yesterday, and to be honest, I think that's where the breakdown of our relationship really began.

I'll tell you something I never told him, though. When I shot that deer, and it bucked up like it did, the only thing I felt was guilt. Here was this beautiful creature hanging out in the woods, running along freely, and I come along with a gun and blow a hole in its stomach. I wonder if the reason I fumbled the slide was because I didn't have the heart to shoot it another time.

Regardless, I never went hunting again.

At least, not for the kind of animals you eat.

At eighteen years old, I was spinning my wheels working odd jobs around the area.

I graduated by the skin of my teeth, applying myself so little that many of the people I've arrested probably have better high-school transcripts than I do. Sadly, I did not become interested in education until it was too late, and I've spent years trying to catch up on all I could have learned, and should have learned, back then.

As a young man with limited prospects, I cleaned carpets and washed windows. I worked as an assistant for the Home and Goods department at Montgomery Newspapers. On weekends I worked at Burkee's Exxon gas station.

I rang the register, changed tires, dispatched tow trucks and pumped gas for customers willing to pay the extra money for full-service. Every morning before I opened the station, I had to measure the gas in the underground fuel tanks with a wooden yard stick. In the wintertime, the ice covering the tanks was so thick I had to smash them open with a heavy metal pike.

On one sunny Sunday afternoon, my entire future would take shape. All it took was one drunk at a gas pump.

I watched this guy pull up to one of the pumps and stumble out of his car. He was staring at the pump like he wasn't sure how to work it and when he started fumbling with the fuel nozzle, gas began leaking onto the parking lot. I had visions of him trying to light a cigarette and blowing all of us up.

I was surrounded by customers in the office area and all of us were watching this happen in mute horror. Nobody had any clue what to do. There we stood, frozen in place, mesmerized by this idiot who was now spraying gas on the sides of his car. Finally, someone said, "Call the cops before that guy hurts somebody."

I dialed 9-1-1 and told the dispatcher where I was and what I was seeing.

"Help is on the way," she said.

Help soon arrived in the form of two marked patrol cars that pulled into the parking lot within minutes. When they rolled in, it was an instant feeling of relief. The good guys were there and everything was going to be okay.

By now, the drunk had gotten the fuel nozzle into his gas tank, but still couldn't figure out how to work the pump. I watched the cops grab this guy by both arms and escort him (drag his ass) into one of the empty garage bays. I remember standing at the register, watching them interview him.

There was a certain way they stood. One of them facing him, the other one vectored off to the side. There was a certain way they spoke. A certain way they looked in their finely-pressed police uniforms and all of the gear they carried.

The drunk couldn't lift his head enough to talk to them. He couldn't look them in the eye.

When I watched those cops put him in handcuffs and drive off, I knew right then what I wanted to do. I wanted to be a police officer. I wanted to be the person people call when they need help.

That August, I enrolled in the Montgomery County Police Academy. My father was so impressed with my decision, he paid the two thousand dollar tuition. That was in 1994. Almost twenty years ago.

In recent years, police departments have gradually shifted toward requiring a college degree. I am probably one of the last generations of police officers where a young person with limited education and prospects could get a job that offers such exceptional benefits and salary.

As I write this now, the decision I made so many years ago has afforded me the opportunity to provide for and raise a family. Like many of you reading this right now, I have mixed feelings about my career. About the toll it takes and the system that governs. However, at the end of the day, being a police officer has allowed me to have a stable job that puts food on the table. It's more than many have, and before I say anything else, I'd just like to make it clear that I was lucky to get hired and feel grateful for the opportunity.

2. Stark Realities

A police officer is being murdered right in front of us. His screams come out of the television and fill the classroom. Every cadet in my Academy class watches this murder happen with wide eyes. Nobody said it would be like this. Nobody said it would be this awful.

In the movies, when people get shot, they die with nobility. They might give a final speech and grab their partner's hand. They might perform some final act of heroism, or tell the people around them to carry on.

That is not what happens in reality, friend. Not by a long shot.

When a person gets shot and it isn't immediately fatal, the scene gets ugly and gruesome fast. There is screaming. There is whimpering. High-pitched, gurgling, pleading, horrible death.

And even if the person that gets shot somehow remains quiet, the people around him certainly do not.

Police officers are all still human. When someone they know is killed, they lose their composure. It doesn't even have to be another person getting killed. One of the videos they showed us was of a K-9 officer who saw his dog get killed. You'd have thought he was watching his firstborn get fed into a meat grinder.

Now, bear in mind that this was all before the days of the internet. In 1994, there wasn't any YouTube and people weren't desensitized by years of reality TV and increasingly outlandish behavior captured by armies of people carrying cellphone video cameras.

The best we had back then was Cops, and they never had an episode where a police officer was just doing his job and wound up getting murdered slowly. I'd never seen anything like it.

For the first time in my life, after growing up in a cop family and being surrounded by cops my entire life, it had never truly occurred to me how truly frightening police work could be.

Our instructor, Mark Flannery, turned off the television and looked around the class. "Do you know what kills cops in most cases when they get shot?"

I lifted my hand. "The bullets, sir?"

There were a few chuckles, but most of the cadets were too attuned to what Mark was saying to pay me any attention. "Panic," he said. "Panic is what kills you. It has been documented that cops shot in non-fatal areas have succumbed to their injuries because they started to panic. 'Oh my God, I got shot!' The heart starts pumping, and the blood starts moving. Next thing you know, it's all pouring out of the wound." He stopped speaking and looked around the class. "And then it's all over. You don't go home. Your kids never see you again. Any good you might have done in this world is cancelled."

"Now," he continued. "There are also been documented cases where cops have survived seemingly fatal injuries and continued to fight out of sheer determination and will-power. Hell no, I'm not going to let you take my life. Say that one with me."

"Hell no, I'm not going to let you take my life!" we repeated.

"I'm going home," he said.

"I'm going home!"

He looked at each of us very carefully. "You might be lying in a pool of your own blood someday. You might be shot to hell and the people who are trying to kill you might be coming your way to finish the job. You get up. You get up and you kill any son of a bitch that wants to stop you from going home to your loved ones, no matter who they are, how bad they are, or how much you are hurt. And that's an order."

I got my first police job in 1997 working part-time at a small borough just outside of Philadelphia. I made ten bucks an hour with no benefits and no vacation time. I was so broke that my car was three different colors of cobbled-together parts and it sometimes emitted a loud banging noise like a gunshot that made people hit the deck when I drove past.

On the day I got hired the Chief opened up a closet in his office filled with old uniforms and said, "Pick out whatever fits you and take it home."

He then handed me a .38 nickel-plated revolver that had electricians tape wrapped around the handle to keep it together. "Don't shoot anybody until you get qualified at the range, kid. Not unless you really, really have to."

I was given two instructions. Do what I was told, and don't show up late.

On my first week of nightwork I was driving to work when my car broke down on a dark street at the bottom of a hill. The headlights started to flicker, the engine light came on, and everything went dark and dead. I couldn't even turn on the hazard lights to warn people they were about to crash into it.

I ran to a house nearby (Yes, this was before we all had cellphones. Yes, I feel old writing this.) and they called 9-1-1 for me. A man named Sergeant James Miller of the Upper Dublin Police Department showed up and said, "You need help?"

We pushed my car through the intersection and off to the side of the road where it was safe. "Do you have someone you want me to call?" he said.

"Can you call my station and let them know I won't be able to make it in?" I didn't say it, but I was pretty sure I was watching my fledgling police career go up in flames.

"Why can't you make it in?" he said.

I shrugged. "They won't come get me this far out of town and I don't have anybody else to give me a ride."

He looked at me like I was crazy. "Get your ass in that police car. There are people relying on you to protect and serve tonight."

Sgt. Miller drove me all the way to work. I told him how grateful I was, and he told me to forget it. "We're cops. It's how things are supposed to be."

On April 20, 2004, at approximately 0415 hours, Sergeant James Miller was killed on-duty responding to an accident.

He was going to help somebody else who needed it, and it cost him his life. I never saw him again after that one night, but you know what? I miss him like hell.

In 2008, on the same night I celebrated my eleventh year in police work, the Detective Sergeant of Upper Gwynedd Township shot himself in the head. He did it at his police station, in the evidence room. He was a thirteen year veteran with a wife and three young children. I never knew him.

Cops do a funny thing when one of their own kills themselves. We right away call him a coward, or a weakling. Something less than we are, as a way to distance ourselves from the horrible fact that if it happened to him it can happen to us.

   That same year, an officer from Doylestown Borough in the neighboring county shot himself in the head. He did it at his home and was found by his two little girls when his ex-wife dropped them off for a visit.

   In 2011, an officer from Upper Southampton (just a few townships down from Doylestown Borough) shot himself while on duty, sitting in his patrol car. The list, unfortunately, goes on and on, and I know for a fact there are some I'm leaving out. Not because I've forgotten them. I just don't have the heart to go digging up the past.

   I remember all the water cooler talk (okay, coffee pot talk) about their various mental conditions and weakness of characters and whatever horrible things they might have done in their personal lives to make suicide look like a good option. Some sort of out we all look for a way to say, "It can't happen to me."

   The reality is, suicide is the dark secret of police work.

These officers get no plaques. There's not black bands worn over our badges to mourn them. Nobody shows up at their funerals dressed in their Class-A uniforms, followed by a horde of motorcycle cops who will escort the casket. In other words, none of the pomp and circumstance of a legitimate police funeral.

Their families won't be celebrated for their heroism, they'll be pitied. Pitied because the cop in their lives was too weak to go on. And personally, I think that is a crock of shit.

Maybe instead of us always asking "What was wrong with that guy?" we should be asking ourselves, "What's wrong with us?"

In the thirty years of my old man's service and my now almost twenty years, I can honestly say it's never been this bad before. Since the year 2000, fourteen Philadelphia Police Officers have been killed in the line of duty. In the past ten years, three were killed in both Bucks County and another three in Montgomery County.

I didn't know any of them.

I miss every single one like hell too.

Everywhere I look, I see broken organizational cultures in Law Enforcement. The old adage is that "If you think it's bad here, you should see what's going on in that department." Well, what if they're all a mess, but also fixable?

The biggest problem with nearly every police organization is that they are imminently fixable. They are within shouting distance of being a great place to work, but they never will be, and it's not because of the budget or the resources or the environment. It is because of a few personalities who run rampant and are dead set against losing their perceived modicum of control.

We all know people in positions of leadership who are more interested in seeing things done their way than the right way, or the easy way, or the intelligent, responsible, sensible way.

And if you dare ask why, the answer will be: Because that's the way we've always done it. The idea is that this has worked for us before, why screw it up?

It's a Herculean task to get a police department to change a single form, let alone their culture, but that doesn't mean it isn't worth trying. The answer is as simple as it is impossible to implement: Everybody stop it with the nonsense and focus on the important stuff.

Good luck with that one, right?

You do not have to be an administrator to be a leader. I realize you may work with people who get ahead by cutting each other's throats, or purposely sabotaging someone when they are on the "fast track." Take it from me, the fast track is a ride that almost always ends in a crash.

Be more interested in learning your job than in what everyone else is doing. Pay attention to your cases and your victims and forget all the petty nonsense that people want to fight over. You might not be the fair-haired child of the Chief, but you will be the one he respects.

Bosses use people who kiss up to them or bring them information. Of course they do. I suppose there's a certain mutual understanding that exists between Master and Supplicant. The Master knows the Supplicant will turn on him at a moment's notice, or that once the Master leaves his position, the Supplicant will forget he existed and go find a new desk to crawl under.

Supplicants, for their part, tend to fight over scraps from the table. They want the new police car, or the special detail, or the whatever-shiny-new-thing they perceive is worth fighting over and lessening themselves for.

You are better than that.

Whether you are a one-day-on-the-job rookie or a forty year veteran, you are better than that and if you're reading this now you are better than that and even if you've been a Supplicant your entire career, you are better than that.

Learn your job. Specialize in the aspects of it that interest you. Become involved with people you can respect and learn from, not the ones who can do things for you.

That is the way of the warrior.

My hope is that for all the road dogs and drug guys who read this book and the Superbia series, and I know it's mainly you because of the emails I get from all around the world asking me if I was secretly writing about their individual police department, a few administrators read a copy as well.

A wise man once told me that people should not seek out advanced positions to increase their personal standing, but to take on more responsibility and effect positive change. Far too often, people use their authority to shield themselves from any possible negative ramifications, rather than actually leading. The word leadership means "to lead" and as far as I know, leading is done from the front. Not the rear. Not from an office. Not from an ivory tower.

The instant bestowing of knowledge and expertise does not come with any rank, just as good judgment and fairness does not come with any badge or gun. If anything, rank and authority bring out the qualities deep within a person, good and bad, simply because they are given greater opportunities to be displayed.

What I want you to take away from this chapter is that it is never too late to improve. If you are a worker, rededicate yourself to improving your knowledge of The Job and staying out of the rat race. If you are a boss, put the needs of your people ahead of your own personal gain, comfort, or past grievances.

3. Training and Equipment

In 1998, I was slashed across the inner left forearm by a box-cutter. The guy swinging the box-cutter was going for my neck and I got my hand up in time to block it. I never saw the box-cutter until after he dropped it on the pavement and ran away.

It had been a last-second instinct that made me get my hand up to block him. That probably saved my life. My arm needed thirteen stitches to get sewn back together and those hours I spent sitting in the emergency room all by myself were the loneliest I've ever felt.

I still have the scar. It reminds me to be careful.

I don't remember blocking his arm, or having a thought that said, "Get your hand up." It was just instinct, born of training. Training is the thing that allows us to function in the middle of chaos. It's the roadmap that leads us out of the wilderness.

It can be the decision between shooting to save a life and freezing up and dying.

I've only ever fired my weapon once in the line of duty, and it will haunt me for the rest of my career. Not because I took the life of another living thing. Because I missed the goddamn dog that was trying to bite me and the cops I work with are relentless pricks.

I responded to a dog bite call and when I showed up there were construction workers standing on their equipment, waving their hands for me to look at a medium-sized terrier running loose nearby. "Careful! It will bite you!" the foreman shouted.

It was winter, and there was snow covering the ground. I pulled on my thickest pair of gloves, thinking that I'd need the extra padding if I tried to grab the dog and it bit me. I parked my car and got out to look for it. That didn't take long.

The second I came out, it charged. It raced over the snow like it had trained for the Iditarod and its jaws were wide open and gnashing. I yelled "Stop!" and tried stamping my foot as hard as I could. It didn't work.

I unsnapped my holster and grabbed my handgun, bringing it up to where I had a direct shot at the animal's chest. "Stop!" I shouted again.

The dog was closing the distance quickly. I moved to pull the trigger, only to realize my stupid godforsaken glove was too thick to fit into the trigger housing. The dog was still coming and I could not shoot.

Finally, just as it was about to jump on me, enough of my glove caught the trigger to pull it. The gun fired, putting a smoking black hole in the ground directly between the dog's feet, missing it by inches. The dog stopped moving instantly.

Everyone and everything around me was strangely silent, right up until one of the construction workers yelled out, "You missed!" And then they all started laughing.

All of a sudden I was twelve years old again, up in that tree stand with my dad.

The dog just stood there and looked at me, cocking its head to the side as if trying to understand what had just happened. After a moment of the two of us looking at one another, it simply turned around and walked back into its house and laid down on the kitchen floor, completely unharmed.

It didn't take long for everybody in my police department to find out what had happened. Cops are brutal. I got drawings of dogs on my desk for months that had targets circled for where to shoot. Cute pictures of puppies saying, "Thank you for missing." That sort of thing. It's been years and they still bring it up. A lot.

As I grow older, I find myself profiling cops everywhere I go.

I watch them the same way a criminal would. Is that cop in good enough shape to fight if something happens? Is he paying attention? Does he see me checking out how he carries his gear?

And out of everything I look for, these are the two most important ones that help me determine if they are ready to deal with a threat. First, does the cop carry a knife, and where does he carry it? Second, are they wearing a bullet-proof vest?

You see a lot of cops carrying knives nowadays, but most of them carry incorrectly. If you ask a majority of police officers why they carry a knife, you'll hear the safe, routine responses. "I carry it for evidence collection, or if I have to cut a seatbelt, or in case someone tries to grab my gun."

All three are absolutely valid. In fact, I believe cops should carry at least one knife, if not two. However, any officer who says "I carry mine in case someone tries to grab my gun" and he is wearing the knife in the pocket under his holster has not really thought this through.

Imagine fighting to keep your gun in your holster while someone is struggling to get it out. Can you really access that knife?

And while you are struggling to keep the gun from coming out and create distance, can't the bad guy just reach under your holster and instead grab your knife?

Personally, I'd rather see you carry the knife off-hand in the opposite pocket, or hidden somewhere on your belt. When the bad guy grabs your gun, use one hand to keep the gun seated and the other hand to eliminate the threat.

I wrote several other things before "eliminate the threat."

You get the idea.

I try to tell guys about this, but most of them just shrug it off. They're cops. They're supermen. It won't happen. And then it does.

It's the same with seat belts and it's the same with bullet proof vests.

Chances are, you will get in your car and drive around on duty and nothing will happen. Right up until it does, and the guy wearing his seatbelt gets out and walks away from the car, and the guy who isn't gets ejected headfirst.

Chances are, you will not get shot while you are on duty. But, if you are shot, and the bullet would have been stopped by a bullet proof vest had you been wearing one, except you didn't because you are too much of an idiot, then don't expect me to have sympathy. Sure, I'll show up at the funeral and feel awful for your family but in the back of my mind, I'll be thinking, "That big, big, dummy."

Unfortunately, I see far too many cops in uniform without a vest on.

I'm not just talking about the old guys, either. We all know cops so old they need two hearing aids and carry a pillow on nightshift "for their back" and they don't wear vests. You can talk to them until you are blue in the face, but it won't make a difference.

I'm talking about the guys under the age of fifty who have no excuse.

If you're one of them, then do me a favor? Stop your police car wherever you are. Put all of your departmental gear in the trunk and lock it. Now call your sergeant to tell him where the car is, and go home.

In fact, go join the post office.

You can still wear a uniform without a vest, you simpleton.

It is inherent that you train with every single piece of equipment you carry.

If you wear a Taser on your left side, you'd better practice drawing it off-hand, taking the safety off, and acquiring a target. When the time comes to really need it (and I mean really need it, not walk up on a job with your Taser already out. I mean the This-Guy-Wants-To-Fight times) you will magically produce the tool you need in order to defend yourself.

Well, not magic. A result of all those times you pulled the car over and got out to practice drawing your weapon, or your knife, or your gun, or your baton.

At the end of the day, when the crap hits the fan, you do what you need to do in order to protect the public, yourself, and affect the arrest. Never give up. If the gun jams and the knife flies out of your hand and the Taser fails and the baton won't engage and your radio is pure static, you have a million other tools at your disposal to get it done. Radios that won't transmit a distress call make a good impact weapon. So do handcuffs, walls, furniture, and anything else you can get your hands on.

People talk about the warrior mindset and the winning mindset and all that other good stuff. I'm a whatever works kind of guy. Adapt, improvise, and overcome. It was true when Mark Flannery said it to us in the Academy back in 1994. It's true now.

And one more thing. If you have big, heavy winter gloves you plan on wearing on duty, it might help to know if you can fire a gun with them on. It helps to know things like that ahead of time. Trust me.

4. The True Blue Line

Police are a modern warrior society.

Not all of us act like it. Some are just in it for the regular paycheck. When it comes down to that dramatic collision between good and evil, you won't see those folks around. They'll be on the other side of town eating a donut, off-radio, oblivious to the fact that you are screaming for help.

There are others who take it very seriously. Some a little too seriously, but still, at least they are dedicated. They are part of the True Blue Line of defense keeping evil at bay. When you are safe at home, with your children sleeping, it is those warriors who are out looking for bad people that want to do bad things to you.

You'll notice I didn't say Thin Blue Line. That's because I don't think its "thin" at all. It's as thick and strong as the last man holding it. Or the last woman. I'd prefer you just say the last cop.

In 2006, the Gallup poll released its annual survey of the public's opinion on the integrity of people performing assorted job functions. Predictably, car salesmen did not fare well. Police officers were ranked in the middle range. I felt that was an appropriate ranking.

On any given week you will see a headline talking about some cop who did something horrendous and is getting locked up for it.

It is a fact that most suburban police officers are young, white, and male. They come from cookie-cutter backgrounds and have normally never dallied with anything remotely close to the darker side of life.

If they weren't squeaky clean, they would have a hell of a time getting a police officer job in the first place.

However, as a society, we then group these kids together, provide them with enormous responsibility and authority, keep them off-balance with irregular sleeping cycles and expose them to lifestyles and cultures with which they have little or no experience dealing with.

What could possibly go wrong?

Actually, I'm amazed more doesn't go wrong. The Gallup Poll indicated that 11% of the public rated police honesty as very low. I completely disagree with that.

Most of the officers I know are extremely dedicated, professional and hard working. They take their responsibilities to heart. With that being said, it is mandatory that we do not allow bad apples into the barrel. When corrupt police officers are found out they must be dealt with quickly and harshly.

Should the Blue Line extend to keeping your mouth shut if you know who posted an unflattering comment about a sergeant on the bathroom wall? Yes it should.

Should the Blue Line extend to letting a guy get some sleep on a midnight shift because he had court that day? Absolutely.

Does the Blue Line extend to me letting a fellow cop break the law? Never.

That is the essence of the True Blue Line. It is a sacred pact held by thousands of men and women in various backgrounds, localities and agencies. It is held by their strength, intelligence, sweat, tears, and sometimes, even their blood.

No one is allowed to cross that line. One hundred percent of the public may not believe in that, but one hundred percent of me does.

I see you nodding your head.

Maybe you've been at the same kind of police funerals I've been to. The ones where everyone is dressed in white gloves and the helicopters zoom overhead. The ones where it's so bitterly cold the trumpets are frozen and the bagpipes don't work.

The ones where a family is dressed in black and someone hands them a folded flag.

It happens. I'm not going to sit here and lie to you that it doesn't happen, but it doesn't stop us. We take the hit and we get back up and we keep holding the line. Why? Because there is nobody else, and if we don't hold it, there would be a hell of a lot more funerals.

The irony is that most of us got into this job to uphold justice, but instead we wind up enforcing the law. These are two very different things. Is it justice, per se, when a single-mother of two living on WIC checks and a minimum wage job has to pay a hundred dollar traffic ticket for blowing a stop sign? No, it isn't. But it is the law, and the law exists to protect children when they are crossing the street at an intersection.

One thing you learn quickly when you get on The Job is that you suddenly become a sounding board for every person you meet who wants to tell you about their single encounter with the police. Here's a tip: Just let them talk.

There is not one person guilty of anything living on the planet today, if you go by their account of things. The people in prison? Didn't do it. The guy you just watched blow through a red light? Never happened. All of this is true, of course, because they will stand there and tell you so.

There are four key words that people normally use when they have just dropped the biggest whopper of a lie in their whole life. They are: "I swear to God."

Did you steal that ring? "No, I didn't. I swear to God."

Did you molest that little kid? "I'm not that kind of person. I swear to God."

It's either them swearing to God, or it's them swearing on the life on one of their loved ones. I've seen it happen. I watched a pregnant mother who was covering up for her thieving boyfriend point at her bulging belly and say, "I swear on the life of my-"

I cut her off. "Just don't say it, lady. Please."

There are moments of true justice to be seen during the course of a police career, and even though they might be few and spaced far apart, they are sweet. They are quiet. It's when you watch a child molester stand in front of a judge and weep because he's going to be a registered violent sexual predator with mandatory neighbor notification for the rest of his life.

It's when you read about an abusive, arrogant, deceitful supervisor who has been charged by the FBI for corruption. It's when you get a hand written card in the mail from one of those kids you got away from a bad situation, telling you that everything is okay now. And saying thanks.

More than likely, they are things no one else will ever know about. The newspapers won't cover the stories, your bosses won't give you a merit award, and you won't get any extra credit for it if you screw up later.

But you'll know. And God knows. And if you ever get the chance to meet him, I hope he says, "Hey. I was watching what you did that time. Nice job."

I often say that it is a true achievement to survive a police career intact. That means 25 years or more of living a clean life. Parties you can't go to because people there will be doing things you can't be associated with. Friends you have to abandon because of decisions they make that you can't support.

It means not doing anything to dishonor yourself, your family, your department, and essentially, every other cop in the world. Because when one falls, we all look bad. 25 years is a long time to live that kind of life, and I am proud of anyone who does it.

I haven't always been right. There are plenty of things I look back on and cringe about. Mistakes I made, that had they gone just a little bit worse, would have resulted in disaster. If I could go back in time and fix them, I would.

But you know what? On a very cold night in 1999 I delivered a baby girl on the floor or her parents' living room.

This tiny little thing came out with the chord wrapped around her neck and she was bright blue. I stuck my finger between the cord and her throat, trying to get it loose enough so that she could breathe. My hands were wet and covered in greasy fluid, and I was trying to keep the baby's head from dropping on the ground. It was all I could do to hold her like that I felt the strong hand of a responding paramedic touch me on the shoulder and say, "It's okay. We've got it from here."

They surrounded her and I stood off to the side, too exhausted to move, feeling like every second that passed was moving me closer to the worst of all possible outcomes. And then, from within that circle of medics, she let out a cry.

I look for her every time I drive down Walnut Street in that Borough. I wonder which little girl she is. She'll never know it, but her life feels like a gift to me.

As a citizen and a father, I trust the police are out there to protect my children, my family, and my loved ones. I trust that when someone I would die for calls 9-1-1, the best in the business are going to show up and resolve the situation. They don't have to be the NYPD. It might just be some cop on a two-man department who takes his job seriously.

As police officers, we took an oath that when there is trouble, we will do whatever is necessary to make things right. That is the true essence of The Way of the Warrior. I didn't invent it. I inherited it from all the older cops I ever knew who held the line long before we ever existed. I'm just writing it here to give it to you.

As a detective, I've gotten used to becoming deeply familiar with the lives of people I've never met. They were already dead. They either overdosed or shot themselves or were murdered.

I had to piece their lives together from photographs and interviews. I had to read letters they wrote to loved ones right before blowing their brains out and splattered the page they were written on.

I make it a rule to not let ghosts haunt me. Sometimes they try. Sometimes I've found myself talking to the dead, trying to tell them things that I wish they'd known when they were alive. But, I guess it is inappropriate for the dead to walk the earth. It is inappropriate for us to be haunted. When the ghosts show up, I pat them on the shoulder and show them the door. My concern is for the living.

Wait a second.
Do you hear that? It sounds like someone screaming.
It's coming from a little girl in that car over there. The one parked behind the shopping center after hours. The one only you would see because you were checking your beat and realized that car didn't belong there. You got off of your butt and investigated it instead of driving past.
On second thought, the screaming is coming from inside that house you just got dispatched to a 9-1-1 hang-up call at. The man who greets you at the door looks annoyed and says, "There's no problem here. I don't know who called."

You don't just take his word for it, though. You go into check around and find a bloody woman in the back bedroom begging you for help.

Hang on. I was wrong again.

It's the child of an about-to-be murdered police officer who is approaching a vehicle he's just stopped. The man inside is a wanted felon with a handgun.

You almost didn't go back up your fellow officer for a second, because you were tired of him constantly calling out with car stops while you were trying to get caught up on paperwork. I think you'd better get over there.

The point is, no one has any idea when you will be given that ultimate call.

The one you were given a badge and gun in the first place, for. The one that God or fate or destiny or whatever you believe drove you to pursue this line of work meant for you to deal with.

Imagine a date marked on your calendar, somewhere along the line, for an event that only you have the power to change. It can happen on your very first day as a snot-nosed rookie. It can happen on your very last day as a washed-up grumpy old-timer.

It can happen when you're making the transition from career cop to full-time author, in which case, you are well and completely screwed.

I am asking you not to let the grinding shifts, the monotony of working the same sector, the captiousness of your supervisors, or the seemingly thanklessness of it all, defeat you. Do not ever give up. Someone, somewhere, desperately needs you.

5. Schaffer's Eight Golden Rules of Criminal Investigation

I've been mentored by some truly, truly great investigators during my career. Older guys who had been around the block and were kind enough to take me under their wing, or maybe just so sick and tired of me bugging them to teach me, and they finally broke down and revealed their inner secrets.

The truth is, not everybody can do criminal investigations.

It takes a certain personality to deal with child molesters, junkies, drug dealers, and all the absolutely horrible people you encounter during investigations. Mainly, you have to accept the fact that people lie.

Let's talk about Joe Cop for a second.

Picture him with his high-and-tight haircut. His I Am the Law mentality. His perfectly shined shoes and sneer of contempt for anyone he meets.

Joe Cop gets a special thrill from writing the most traffic tickets. Joe Cop gets suspiciously aroused at the idea of punishing others. I am quite sure Joe Cop used to spend a lot of time in school being picked on, and now it's his turn to make the world pay.

One thing Joe Cop knows is the difference between right and wrong. Basically, he is right and you are wrong. Joe Cop is not particularly used to, or good at, talking to people. Sure, he talks at them, but the biggest part of any successful interview and interrogation is listening.

I have watched Joe Cop literally stop a person from confessing, just because he needed to make one more point.

This is the height of idiocy.

A police officer investigating a crime who is on the brink of getting a confession stops the bad guy from talking, just so he can say get one final point in.

Somewhere out there, some of you reading this are laughing your asses off because you know exactly what I'm talking about. It doesn't matter if you work in Philadelphia or London, the police world is full of the types of people who belong on a highway running speed details and nowhere near an interview room.

The fine art of interview and interrogation is not for everyone.

I've watched cops in interviews take out their cellphones and start sending text messages to their girlfriends. I've watched FBI agents pull newspaper articles out of their briefcases to show suspects about some big arrest they made. I've watched a former Chief of Police take out a Bible and conduct an impromptu sermon on a suspect, talking about the demons within.

I've seen all sorts of bizarre and unprofessional things investigators have done, all in an effort to prove to the public at large that they don't deserve to hear them confess.

But the worst, the absolute worst, thing an interviewer can do is hand someone a blank sheet of paper and say, "Write a statement," then take that statement back and say, "Thanks for coming in."

And that's it.

In other words, Joe Cop's boss told him, "Get a statement."

Joe Cop got a statement.

He didn't read it, didn't ask any questions, didn't give it a second thought.

"Der, I got you that statement, boss."

Good job, Joe. Now get back on the highway and make us some money.

I'm not saying you have to be a handwriting analyst, or an expert in the Reid method, or anything like that. There are multitudes of interviewing schools available to the interested person, and while I do not subscribe to the theory that any single one of them is a silver bullet to unlocking the mysteries of interviewing, you can probably gain something from each of them.

The best interview school I ever went to, believe it or not, was for Hostage Negotiation.

As a hostage negotiator, I learned the single most important question you can ask a person in that situation is, "How did we get here?"

It's also the best possible question you can ask any suspect, regardless of what brought them to your door.

People want to talk. They want to be heard. They want to give their side of the story. They want someone to listen to all the misfortunes and comedy of errors that led them to this moment in time when you are looking at them across from a table in a police interrogation room.

Remember, the junkie you are disgusted by does not see themselves as junkie. In fact, they're not "a junkie." They are a person. They had a childhood and parents and dreams and even if heroin has rotted out their insides from stem to stern, there is still someone in there who believes they are better than the actions that brought them to you.

One thing I've always secretly believed is that if my life had just gone slightly differently, if I hadn't decided to go into the police academy, if I hadn't been rescued by getting a full-time job when I did, I have no idea what I would have turned into.

Aside from the child molesters and a few really despicable people I've encountered, I've never believed I was better than someone I arrested. Had better impulse control? Sure. Made better decisions? Absolutely. Smarter than? Sometimes. But not better than.

It's a concept Joe Cop can't wrap his head around. It would involve too much self-analysis and challenge all those concrete ideas he's got about right and wrong.

In my experiences, most people you will deal with as a criminal investigator are not "bad people." There's very little stone-cold evil in the world, anyway. And when you do come across it (You will) they won't see themselves as the bad guys anyway. That's when you really need to listen. Evil people are generally narcissistic and prone to either glorifying themselves or portraying the victim. Either way, they will tell you what you want to know as long as you are able to be patient and listen and not let them know how much you want to dig out their eyeballs with a dull spoon.

So, onto my Golden Rules of Criminal Investigation. Hang on. A little caveat before we get started.

The reason they are called Schaffer's Golden Rules is because that is exactly what they are. They are my preferred rules, as I both observed others and practiced the police trade over a certain period of time. They are not called "the" Golden Rules because I would never be so deluded as to think I had all the answers. I don't. Many of you reading this book have police experience that dwarfs mine, and I don't pretend to be nearly as qualified as you.

This is what has worked for me.

If I missed some that you believe should be included, drop me a line. If you disagree with something I say, I'm all ears. You are welcome to use anything you find in this book that applies to you and toss the rest out like yesterday's newspaper. You are welcome to skip this part entirely. You are welcome to write your own rules and publish them as you see fit.

I don't think I'm too far off, though. Let me know how I do.

Rule Number One: The Truth Must Make Sense

It seems so obvious, and yet you'd be amazed how many people fall for the silliest explanations. They let someone's sincerity convince them that whatever line of cockamamie nonsense they just laid down must really be the truth. It isn't. The truth rings like a bell, and it almost always makes logical sense.

If someone is giving you an account of an event, I don't care if they are a victim, witness, suspect, prospective employee, or fellow cop. If what they are saying doesn't make sense, take a real, real hard look at what that person is telling you, because chances are, it's bogus.

Now, this is not to say that people aren't strange. This is not to say that people won't tell you about bizarre decisions they made or circumstances that you cannot believe a sane person would become involved in. However, you must consider the person and their frame of mind.

Facts can be very hard to twist and turn and obfuscate to fit into fiction.

Probably the best example I can think of in terms of this would be the JonBenet Ramsey case.

I'm not going to go into details about the case here because it would take too long, but let's discuss one simple aspect of the investigation.

Does it make sense that a rough draft of the ransom note was found inside the parents' house?

If your answer to that is no, then you have no other alternative than to immediately begin focusing your investigation on the people in that house. Period.

If your answer is anything other than no, congratulations. You have a promising future in the postal service and should begin making preparations with all due haste.

Rule Number Two: Write Court-Oriented Reports

Investigative reports do not reflect an investigator's opinion or conclusion. They are impartial observations of events as they occur. Period.

Unfortunately, most police reports are used as some sort of job-justification, or meant to impress the bosses at how really, really, really hard you worked that day finding the phone number for a witness.

All your reports are discoverable by the defense, and therefore should only contain elements of the investigation that pertain to the charges filed.

Also, they should not ever (And I mean EVER) contain police techniques used to perform an investigation. Not if you ever intend on using them again, that is.

Inexperienced cops are like James Bond villains, in that sense. They can't wait to tell the audience exactly how their big scheme unfolded and gloat over how it actually worked. Congratulations, dummy. Your criminal complaint just gave your defendant, his attorney, and all their buddies a blueprint to study and plan to defeat next time.

Rule Number Three: Develop Suspects Organically

A fatal flaw in any investigation is that the investigator begins with a belief as to who the criminal is and structures his case to support that theory. Your suspect should develop naturally out of the results of your interviews, evidence, and findings.

I often use Jack the Ripper as a perfect example of people trying to shoehorn in a preconceived suspect to fit a crime. People have made good money writing books and filming TV shows how Jack the Ripper was a Freemason, a member of the Royal Family, Lewis Carrol, Walter Sickert, William Gull, and more.

The problem is they are drawing names out of hats (normally famous, attention-getting names) and trying to use enough circumstantial evidence to say, "Eureka! I've got him!"

It's like taking a puzzle piece and forcing it into place. A bad idea.

Always let the evidence and statements and interviews direct you toward a suspect. All that matters is what you can prove in the court of law. Nothing else. Not your theories, not your suspicions, not your prejudices and beliefs. Can you prove beyond a reasonable doubt that the person sitting at the defendant's table is guilty of the crime you are accusing him of? If so, then you've done your job. If you arrested someone because of an early suspicion you had and your entire case is built around shoehorning the facts to convict that person, you have done the entire criminal justice system a disservice.

Rule Number Four: Theories are for Television (And Desk Jockeys)

With any major case, you'll run into the "what if" people. These are the folks who listen to the circumstances of the crime you are investigating and want to reiterate all the wonderful things they've heard on television.

The "what if" people will offer you theories out the wazoo, and none of it will be useable in court. If we're playing the "what if" game, Alien Abduction and KGB Hit Squads can only be a few short leaps of logic (?) away.

Just as what people are telling you must make sense, and you develop your suspects organically, your evidence will indicate one clear explanation for the event. Do not waste your time tracking down imaginary theories concocted by people with nothing better to do.

This does not mean you will not be questioned by a defense attorney at some point as to whether or not you checked all possible angles. Here's how you handle that. You tell the truth.

"Did you call the Men in Black to see if they were in the area that day?"

"No, I did not."

"Did you call the CIA to see if they were responsible for the murder in connection to the Tri-Lateral Commission?"

"No, I did not."

"Well why not?"

"Because I had no reason to. The investigation dictated a path that led me to your client."

Stay calm, tell the truth, and don't get suckered into the what-if game, whether it's by defense attorneys or bosses.

Rule Number Five: Mirandize Only When Necessary

To be an effective interviewer and interrogator, you must (MUST!) have a firm understanding of Miranda, and when it applies. A lot of people don't. For Miranda Warnings to apply, meaning that you must advise someone of their rights, two standards must be met. Not one of them. Not one and a half. Two, at the same time. They are:

1. The person must be (or believe themselves to be) in custody.
2. They be asked guilt-seeking questions.

That's it.

Some interviewers are too scared of their own shadows to not Mirandize, and some departments are too backwards to understand it, but only when those two conditions are met must we Mirandize someone.

I have watched cops stop someone from spontaneously confessing and say, "Before you say anything else, I need to read you your rights."

I have watched cops stop someone from confessing in order to re-Mirandize the suspect, just to make sure they really, really, really understood they had a right to remain silent.

You cannot be an effective interviewer unless you possess a clear and firm understanding of Miranda, but the good news is, you only need to remember two things to have one.

Are they in custody, or do they believe they are in custody?

Am I asking them guilt-seeking questions?

The obvious pitfall is proving whether or not someone believed they were in custody?

Actually, the answer is quite easy. You tell them.

The moment you bring the subject into your police station you say, "You understand you are not in custody and are free to leave at any time, correct?"

As long as he says he understands, begin your interview and document that you told him.

Rule Number Six: Be an Expert Interrogator

Whole college courses could be taught on the fine art of interviewing and interrogation and it still would not cover everything, so I can't expect to possibly convey all that you need to know in these few short pages.

To be completely honest, I don't subscribe to any particular methods of interviewing. I'm not a Reid disciple nor a devotee of neuro-linguistics or tricks and I don't buy into that crap that a guy who puts his head down in the interview room is automatically guilty. I believe in polygraph examiners and not so much in polygraph machines. Any techniques I use have evolved and changed over the years through simply talking to people and observing masters of the craft.

In the old days, guys like my dad used to carry around fingerprint cards in their hats and when they were trying to get a confession from someone, they'd whip out that card and go, "Oh, really? Then why was your fingerprint found at the crime scene!"

I would die of embarrassment if I had to do that. I'm not a fan of tricks or traps or any of that greasy kid stuff, really. I stick to the basics. I listen during the interview segment and yell during the interrogation segment. Easy as pie.

Here are a few brief tips to get you on your way.

I prefer to do interviews alone, in a quiet area. I keep a pen and notepad close at hand, but out of sight of the subject.

While they speak, I am completely devoted to everything they say. I'm not texting, writing, or talking to anyone else. You are taking your life in your hands if you walk into the room while I'm conducting an interview. It's that serious.

I generally begin the interview by asking the subject what happened. This gives them the chance to spew out whatever monologue they've been practicing for days. It's when they give off their big explanation, and gives you a chance to see what they're all about. I imagine that if I had committed a crime and the police were calling me in to discuss "something" I would practice my explanation. I'd have my story down pat by the time I walked in. I'd be so focused on what I was going to say that it would be all I could think about.
   But that would probably be the extent of the gas I had in my tank.
   When an interviewer lets the person say whatever it is they've prepared right off the bat, it takes the air out of their tires quickly. That's when you should be paying careful attention to their story, mentally matching it up to the details you already possess.
   Chances are, you know if you're talking to the right person after this stage.

As every police cadet knows, the interview stage is when you ask questions. The interrogation stage is when you provide information. Let me up your game a little bit. Where most cops fail during the interview stage is they give away too much information. They play their hand too early and give the subject a chance to counter anything else you hit them with.

Remember to structure your questions in a way that does not reveal anything about your investigation.

Interviewing someone is a fact-finding mission. They are providing you with all the little pieces of information that you are going to need when you start blowing their story apart.

However, there is one vital piece of information that you must acquire during the interview stage: Find out what your suspect loves, and what he is afraid of.

For some, it's being exposed. A pedophile might be the sickest piece of trash you've ever seen, but he will do anything for the people at his church not to find out. Or his wife. Or his work.

For others, it may be the loss of a professional license, or the opportunity to work in their field again after they are arrested.

Regardless, it is a question should have an answer to by the time your interview phase comes to an end. Once you have determined what makes your interview subject tick, you are ready to begin the interrogation.

The interrogation phase sounds simple. You provide information. Let me clarify. You bombard the subject with overwhelming facts that offer them no opportunity for escape. Quickly blast them with whatever you have that connects them to the crime. Let them know in no uncertain terms how you are going to show your evidence to the judge and jury and let them decide if they believe the facts of the case, or the bullshit story the defendant came up with.

People will get indignant and ask to see the evidence.

Tell them you only show evidence in the courtroom.

People will want to examine the facts of what you know in order to decide if you have enough to deserve their confession.

Tell them they can read the facts in the warrant you are about to go get.

Tell them that right now the only thing that can stop you and a dozen of your friends from the SWAT team from coming to kick their door in is a real, truthful, honest explanation of how things went so goddamn wrong in their lives that they wound up here.

And then, for the love of God, shut your mouth.

Just wait.

I call it The Silence.

It's the moment when both sides have stopped talking. It's the moment when your interview and interrogation has reached critical mass.

This is when the pretenders blow it and the professionals succeed.

It is an exercise in self-control, because absolutely under no circumstances are you to be the one who breaks the silence. Look at them. Don't let them escape your stare. Try and imagine what is going through the subject's mind, what gears are grinding away. They are weighing the odds right now. They are trying to decide if it's worth it to continue lying, knowing that those lies are going to result in jail time, or are they going to tell the truth and ask you for help.

Don't move.

Don't look away. Keep staring at them and keep waiting.

It makes people crazy.

They can't stand it that uncomfortable silence. They'll confess just to get you to stop staring at them.

Keep waiting.

Most of the times, they are going to finally spit it out.

When they do finally sputter out the truth, make sure you tell them you appreciate how hard it was for them to tell you the truth, because really, it is. And right now, they are feeling a certain type of relief or euphoria that it is finally over. Now it is time to move forward.

At some point a suspect is going to say, "What can you do to help me?"

Good question. Was this all just smoke and mirrors to get a confession so we can ram it down their throats at court? I'd prefer you said no, because I try never to lie to someone. They will remember it, and they will tell people, and it generally hampers your effectiveness in the future. I tell people the truth, even when it's not necessarily pretty.

My response to people when they ask me what I can do for them is usually the same. It also happens to be what I personally believe.

"People understand when someone makes a mistake, as long as they own up to it. If you can stand up and say, "I made a mistake, and I'm willing to do what it takes to fix it," the world will open its doors to you.

Judges and probation officers and family members and everyone else will rally to help you. The prisons are already too full with people who couldn't admit they needed help, so we had to put them in a special place designed to teach people the difference between right and wrong.

Admitting you need help shows that you understand that difference and are willing to try and make it right, starting today. If you ask for it, I will make sure everybody knows you deserve it. Do you want help?"

And again, let that sit.

At this point, you are the only friend in the world this person has. You know the absolute worst thing they've ever done in their lives, and you haven't judged them. You offered them help.

Is it hard to be nice to a person who just admitted to molesting a child?

Of course it is. Goes against everything we know to be right and true in this world.

However, I'm asking you to see beyond that initial revulsion and consider this: Who are you actually helping? By gleaning a confession from a child molester, you are lessening the chances of that victim having to testify exponentially.

No trial, no defense attorney, no further trauma by the system.

Is it hard on you as a police officer and a human being?

Damn straight.

Is it worth it?

Damn straight.

If your department doesn't record their interviews, you will have to get the confession in writing. This is the time when you now have to transition from angry Pentecostal minister threatening the fiery pits of hell for all those who don't repent, to Mother Theresa, the kind and loving savior of all who ask for mercy.

I used to get written statements from people by handing them a sheet of paper and saying, "Write all that stuff down that you just said."

I finally got tired of reading, "I dun all dat bad stuff me an' dis detective talked abowt."

So, I got wise and began writing out Question and Answer forms with suspects, where I wrote down carefully crafted questions that normally required only a Yes or No answer.

At the very top of your page, the first question should always be, "Do you understand you are not in custody and free to leave?"

Then, structure your questions using the details they've provided, while giving them the chance to answer in simple terms. Example: Is it true you told me that on Friday, June 5th, you went into your living room and raped your parakeet?

Then write Yes or No (Circle One) underneath it.

After I've established the facts of the case and confession, I give the person a chance to expand on some of the personal things they told me. I'll ask them about their drug addiction or history of being abused or financial troubles. It gives the person a chance to explain themselves, and also shows you weren't just screaming and yelling at the suspect the entire time. You took the time to learn about them as people, and gave them the opportunity to plead their case.

Does it excuse what they did? Absolutely not. But always remember it is not our job to portray people as either innocent or monstrous. Our only job is to tell the truth and present the facts.

My final question on every Q and A is always, How did the police treat you today?

In all these years I've only ever had one person say I threatened them into confessing. The defense attorney came up to me in the courthouse lobby and said how he was going to do this and that because his client told him how I'd threatened him into confessing.

I reached into my case file, pulled out the Q and A and said, "Read that last question, sir."

He looked at where I'd written "How did the police treat you today?" and then at the place his client had written, "Good" and then they waived the hearing and plead.

Rule Number Seven: Always Tell the Truth, Even When it is Unflattering

Cops get jammed when they don't want to admit something got screwed up. Listen to me very carefully. No case is worth lying for. It is better to lose a case on a technicality by far than to win it by glossing over some screwy fact.

Things happen, especially when you are dealing with informants, evidence, suspects, and complicated rules and procedures. The judicial system can tolerate mistakes, as long as they aren't malicious and as long as they are documented and owned up to.

What the judicial system cannot tolerate, nor should it tolerate, is a Law Enforcement official lying. It stains the entire process and creates distrust for police that will have widespread consequences.

Most of the cops who bend the rules will justify it by saying, "There are too many rules to begin with."

Well, how do you think they got that way? Probably more than a few were created to protect the citizenry from cops who were either too lazy to follow the rules, or who lied.

That includes lies of omission, fabrications of probable cause, and all the stupid stuff confidential informants did, despite being instructed otherwise. If, at the end of the day, the bad guy walks on a technicality and all you did was cost him the price of an attorney and a few buckets of sweat, so be it.

Here's a secret about bad guys. They always come back. You'll get another bite at the apple, and the next time around, you'll have learned from your mistakes enough to put a serious hurting on him.

Do not jeopardize your career, your honor, your reliability, or the public belief that police officers can be believed, by cutting corners. It is the height of hypocrisy and the road to ruin.

Rule Eight: Do Not Educate Anyone

Dealing with informants for drug cases is a whole other book in itself, and one I'll eventually get around to writing, but the number one rule for dealing with informants can also be applied to everybody else you deal with. Do not educate them.

Do not tell victims what you are doing in the investigation, no matter how much they bug you.

Do not tell bad guys how you cleverly caught them, or what evidence you have on them, unless you already have enough to charge them.

Do not tell defense attorneys how you operate.

The sad reality is that the victim you are feeding information to might accidentally be telling your suspect how close the police are in their investigation. Not because they think it's the suspect. Because they never dreamed their cousin would steal their jewelry, or their babysitter is the one slashing their tires and sending them death threats.

The informant you are getting along with so well today is going to be the drug target you work tomorrow. Keep them out of sight and hearing distance of the operation.

And one more thing.

As much as it pains me to say it.

Do not educate your fellow cops about what you are working on, unless they are actively involved. You'd be amazed (also depressed, horrified, and angered) at how many cops let slip a detail about an investigation to the wrong person. Not on purpose. Drinking at a bar. Trying to impress a girl. Talking to their hairdresser who secretly knows the suspect and is going to immediately reach out to them.

Spare them, yourself, your department, and everybody else the complications and keep people on a need to know basis.

A word to the wise: This will not make you popular.

In fact, very little of what you do as a criminal investigator will make you popular with the rank-and-file. Or the bosses of the rank-and-file.

Dems de breaks, kid.

It comes with the job.

6. The Unsolvable Problem with Police Work (A Starter Guide)

I know many of you came to this chapter with a slight roll-of-the-eye. A smirk. The phrase, "Go ahead and tell me something I don't know" escaping from the cynical depths of your being.

Maybe I will.

There are two problems with police work that appear to be unsolvable, at least from a single organization's perspective and certainly, the individual officer. And just to show you how I rank the two in terms of priority, I'll address the individual officer first.

First, police work is filled (and I mean FILLED, busting at the seams, even) with highly-qualified, highly-trained, extremely experienced individuals. Think about all the categories of expertise any given officer in any given agency possesses: Crime Scene, Narcotics identification, Drug Labs, Computer Forensics, K-9, Truck Inspection, Firearms instruction, Defensive Tactics, and more. The list goes on forever.

Police officers in this day and age are as trained and qualified as any professional in any field. But they are hamstrung by one major difference.

If you dedicate your life to becoming a master mechanic, you will spend years learning your trade, acquiring certifications, and developing your skills to the point that you can work in any shop you choose. If you get a job at Bob's Autobody and come to realize that everybody who works at Bob's (including Bob) is a scumbag, you can pack up your tools and go work at Floyd's Motors. Easy.

The difference in police work is that your skills and certifications pertain to your agency alone. Sure, you can quit and go work for another police department, but you start at the bottom. Low man on the totem pole. Back to starting salary, back to the bottom of the seniority food chain.

Let's face it. Nobody is going to be able to call the NYPD and say, "Hey, got any openings in Homicide? I'm thinking about coming to work there." In fact, not only will you not laterally transfer in based on your level of experience or expertise, you will more than likely have to go back through the Police Academy.

There are, at least, some states around the country that offer the ability to transfer pensions or offer some greater ability to laterally transfer in terms of rank and vacation time. They are, to be certain, the minority. Police who work for larger agencies have the option to transfer to completely different divisions, troops, precincts and units. They can also be summarily transferred against their will.

Working for a police department is essentially the same as getting married at an early age. You think it's for the best, but have no idea what your spouse is going to be like five, ten, fifteen years from now.

Police work looks pretty good from the outside, though. Steady job, nice benefits, respectable means of making a living, and a chance to serve and protect.

That's why police jobs are hard to come by. They involve a test fee, competitive written and physical exams, a series of stress-inducing interviews, polygraphs, psychological exams, and background investigations.

You compete against hundreds of people just to scratch and claw your way to the top of that heap and hear the words, "We'd like to offer you a position with our agency."

Strange organizational culture? I don't care, as long as I have a job.

No tested promotions, just temporary assignments? I don't care, as long as I have a job.

History of uneven discipline and favoritism? I don't care, as long as I have a job.

And that was all true for me, and is probably true for every single one of you reading this right now. The problem comes in down the road, when you're a spoke in the wheel and realize you've spent decades trapped in the same cycle. When you realize that you cannot get out.

I know for a fact that there are some of you out there as highly-qualified as any lawyer or accountant or master carpenter. It troubles me that you'll never have the same opportunities though.

Unless you're a Chief.

That's kind of funny how that works, isn't it? People who run police agencies somehow seem to possess the magical ability to go from one agency to another and run it no matter what. Detectives couldn't investigate somewhere else, sergeants couldn't supervise, lieutenants couldn't oversee a platoon, and highway officers couldn't put on their big boots and go ruin the local economy by enforcing piddly little traffic offenses to generate revenue.

Sorry, I got distracted.

Only Chiefs and Commissioners can, with all their vaunted experience, transfer from agency to agency with all their gold eagles and stars intact. Everybody else has to start over as a runt rookie.

How amazingly convenient.

Police organizations, and probably all public sector jobs, suffer from an unsolvable problem that puts them on the short end of the stick compared to the private sector. It all comes down to performance.

In the private sector, there's a clear, definitive way of measuring success: Money.

If your company makes money, you're doing something right. If you need better equipment to make more money, chances are you'll get it. If somebody works in your company who is hurting your chance of making money, he'll probably get fired or taken out of that position.

What standards do we use to measure performance in police work?

Traffic tickets.

Homicide rates.

Crime statistics.

Let's use Philadelphia as an example. Philadelphia had 331 murders in 2012. That's up from the 324 in 2011, and way up from the 306 in 2010.

Oh my God. What can the police do to stop this awful trend?

The answer is: Not much.

First off, the cops cannot control whether or not a person is going to kill someone else unless we are there when it happens. The solution, people would argue, is that by cleaning up the streets and taking away the illegal weapons, we can stem the tide of all these murders.

The only way to do that is by cracking down.

The cops will send in the stormtroopers to stop everyone they see and pat them down and take their guns and drugs and rough them up and inflate the stats way, way up.

Crime will go down.

Temporarily.

Soon, all those cases are going to hit the courts, and it's going to create an absolute logistical nightmare. And once people aren't so upset about the skyrocketing crime rates, they're going to realize they don't like the idea of the police harassing them non-stop day and night. That's when the civilian oversight committees will come in, the lawsuits will fly, and the individual officers will be scrutinized.

It's a lose-lose situation, filled with temporary fixes and band aids.

It doesn't have to be anything as serious as homicides, however. It can be something as simple as a speeding complaint on a residential street. Old Lady Mary calls her local police department to complain about all the speeding vehicles in front of her house. The cops come, sit in her driveway for a few days and write some tickets. She feels good about the increased enforcement, the cops chalk it up to another victory and everybody moves on.

We all know that the problem of speeding vehicles has not been stopped. We all know, as rational human beings that writing a few traffic tickets will not prevent cars from flying up and down her street a few days after the cops leave.

But that's how it's done. In the public sector, a problem is fixed once someone stops complaining about it.

Since there is no accurate way to measure success in the public sector, it's difficult for agencies to promote people who will make the organization more successful. In most profit-driven companies, the guy running things has a long and proven track record of getting things done. He helped the company be successful in the past and now he's going to manage and inspire others to do the same.

We all know that's not the case in the public sector.

In police work, the best way to move up is to not do anything. Why? Because the more active you are, the more likely your chances of getting involved in a messy situation become. Was it messy because of your involvement? Probably not. It was just your luck of the draw that you happened to be the cop that showed up.

The more messy the situation, the more likely the chances of there being complaints and lawsuits and ramifications. Entries into your personnel file. Headaches for the bosses. That sort of thing. And as we all know, bosses are not keen on promoting people who cause headaches.

The sad truth is that you are better off following orders, doing what's required, keeping your head down, staying out of trouble, and studying hard for the next promotional exam if you want to get ahead. Take a nice, even approach to your career and avoid drama that goes on inside the station.

You should be just fine. In fact, maybe someday you will have the chance to run an agency and implement some of the things you'd always wished for. It would be my sincerest hope that you are able to rise as high as you can while maintaining your dignity, honor, and sense of duty to the public and your fellow officers.

Oh, and whatever you do, don't get the idea that you should be writing books about fictional police departments that people think is a clear reflection of the one you actually work for. That just leads to trouble.

7. Back to the Start

I get some really cool emails from people. Cops who read the earlier edition of Way of the Warrior or the SUPERBIA books tend to reach out to me and share their own experiences. I'm glad they feel like my voice is theirs. I don't pretend to speak for Law Enforcement or other Police Officers, but if some of the people out there feel like I'm communicating what they are going through, it's an honor and a privilege.

I hope my work leaves people with not just a sense of the burden of The Job, but also some of the fun we have along the way. One of my favorite scenes in SUPERBIA is where Vic, the seasoned investigator, is showing his new partner Frank how to go through someone's trash for evidence. Of course, nothing is ever that easy.

Vic slid his hands into leather gloves, then pulled a pair of latex gloves over the top of them. "I can touch anything in the world if I'm set up like this, okay?" He picked up the trash bag and took it outside, making sure to set it down beneath the overhead light. He pulled out a knife from his pocket and flicked it open with one hand, then slit the bag lengthwise. "Bring another bag over here and hold it open."

Frank put on his gloves the same way that Vic had and held the bag open, keeping his face as far from the bag as possible. Vic reached into the first trash bag and pulled out a rolled up diaper that was leaking brown fluid onto the asphalt.

"Nobody in their right mind would open this. Drug dealers count on that." Vic peeled off the sticky tape holding the diaper together and unrolled it. "Oh boy. What did they feed this kid. That's disgusting."

Frank looked down and gagged. "Hurry up, roll it back up and put it in here."

Vic dropped the diaper in and reached back for another. "Only four more to go."

Frank buried his face into his bicep and tried crushing his nostrils against the fabric. His eyes watered from the fumes and odor of liquid feces. The sticky side of the tape got caught on Vic's rubber glove and he struggled to get it open without spilling the contents of the diaper onto the two of them. He slowly unrolled the diaper and said, "There. You see that?"

Frank opened one eye and looked sideways down at the diaper without moving his face away from his arm. "What is that?"

"It's a plastic bag." Vic laid the diaper down and spread it out on the ground. He picked up a stick and poked the brown liquid inside, using the tip of the stick to hoist a glassine sandwich bag out of the soup. "Here, take a look at this."

Frank pinched his nose and squatted down beside him.

"This is a source bag," Vic said. "It's the one the cocaine comes in. If you look close, you can still see chunks of it at the bottom."

"The only chunks I see are baby corn shit."

Vic squeezed the bag flat between his gloved fingers to show him the minuscule pieces settled at the bottom of the bag. "This is big enough for an ounce of raw coke. The dealer probably stepped on it enough to turn that into two or maybe two and a half."

"What does stepping on it do, squish it?"

Vic turned to look at him. "Are you serious? Didn't you ever watch The Wire?"

Frank shrugged. "I don't watch TV."

"It's the single greatest cop show since Homicide or NYPD Blue."

"Never saw them either."

Vic flinched and said, "How the hell can you be a cop and not have watched them? It's basic training."

"What do they have to do with what I do out here?"

Vic shook the bag and said, "Maybe if you watched them, you'd know what this..." he stopped speaking and his voice turned into a small squeak in his throat. His eyes widened in horror.

"What?" Frank said.

"Dude, don't move."

"Why?"

"It's nothing. Just don't move." Vic set the bag down and said, "I'll be RIGHT back. Just stay there."

Frank grabbed him by the arm, "Tell me what's happening!"

"Get your hand off my shirt! You were just digging through trash!"

"Tell me and I'll let go."

Vic lowered his voice and said, "You have a small, teeny, tiny piece of baby poop on your cheek. Real close to your lip. For the love of God, don't move. I'll get a towel and we'll wipe it off."

Frank's eyes widened and his jaw quivered slightly. The quiver turned into a full blown spasm as he leapt to his feet and screamed, "You son of a bitch! You got shit on me!" Frank grabbed the wet diaper off of the ground with his hand and cocked it over his shoulder like a football.

"It was an accident!" Vic shouted as he jumped back and threw his hands over his face. "Hey! Hey! That diaper is evidence! Do not throw it, Frank. It has evidence and I am giving you a direct order to put it down."

"You are so dead," Frank hissed.

"Put it down, Frank. Let's both calm down."

"That is easy for the guy with no shit on his face to say!"

"The more you talk the closer that shit gets to falling right into your…oh Jesus. Where did it go?"

"What?" Frank said.

"I don't see it anymore. Christ…I think with all your moving and yelling it might have…we'd better get you inside."

"In my mouth?" Frank shrieked. He dropped the diaper and stuck his tongue out and wagged it like a dog, spitting everywhere.

Vic watched Frank take off running around the parking lot, screaming. "Frank? You okay buddy?"

Frank bent over and clutched his stomach, ready to dump its contents. "Get the hell away from me!"

"Ok," Vic said, patting him on the back. "Just let it out. There you go. That's better, buddy. That's right."

Ah, the good old days.

Since the publication of the first Way of the Warrior essay, a lot has changed for me regarding police work. I am no longer a detective or a member of the narcotics unit. I'm back on patrol pushing a marked car around, working shift work, just like most of them.

Maybe just like you, who is reading this right now.

I can't really go into details as to why it happened, but enough has been written about it already that people know I was stripped of the rank due to SUPERBIA and a promotional video on YouTube. The video is a poem I wrote called "Wait and Wait" about working a narcotics job.

I've said before that I have no regrets. That I made a conscious decision to pursue writing in lieu of the current position I was in. That I was willing to sacrifice whatever I had to in order to be true to my craft.

That's still pretty true, for the most part, but I'd be lying if I said I didn't miss it. There have been a few instances where I've had to put my investigator hat back on. It's like an old flame that you never get over.

After all that time working in detectives, there are aspects of the job I'm highly skilled at but will likely never get the chance to use again. There're many other aspects I'm probably less useful at than a two-month rookie. It's not my fault. In the seven years I missed of being on patrol they got all these newfangled computers and other fancy stuff I never saw before.

The reality is, I doubt I will remain a police officer for very much longer.

Writing has been a successful venture for me, and given how much I've sacrificed in order to do it, it's a little late to go back now. To press on seems the only logical choice.

I think the final lesson police work has taught me, and that I can offer you here, is that who you are as both a person and a police officer, isn't based on your rank or your job. That all comes to an end. If your whole persona is based on being a detective, or a drug cop, or a highway guy, or a Chief, or whatever else, the reality is that it is going to go away.

Someone else will have to take up both that position and responsibility. Guys who can't let it go tend not to do well in retirement. Or, even worse, they tend not to retire. They lurk around their respective departments like poltergeists, staunchly refusing to get out of the way for anybody else.

The first book I ever wrote was WHITECHAPEL: THE FINAL STAND OF SHERLOCK HOLMES. I intended it to be a realistic portrayal of the Jack the Ripper killings as they happened, with the inclusion of characters from the Arthur Conan Doyle's stories. As I researched the book, I came across a biography written in 1931 by a chief constable of the Scotland Yard Criminal Investigation Department.

Frederick Porter Wensley was just a rookie with the Metropolitan London Police Department in 1888, and one of his first assignments was to walk the beat in Whitechapel to try and catch Jack the Ripper. Wensley later went on to become the Chief of CID and the most decorated investigator in the history of Scotland Yard.

His book, FORTY YEARS OF SCOTLAND YARD, absolutely stunned me. Despite the fact we were from two wildly different time periods and countries, he and I basically felt the same about police work.

The Job truly never changes.

Technology marches on and the faces change, but at the end of the day, what we're doing now is no different than what any other generation has done before us. How we feel about The Job and the people we work for and with is no different than it was for Constable Wensley when he was out walking the beat in Whitechapel.

For as much as The Job itself hasn't changed, it certainly changes the people who do it. And the people who do it change as well. In my time, I've seen so many cops come and go it's hard to keep track of them all.

Countless people who were police officers from the time I started have been fired, died, retired, quit, or arrested. The ones I find most unique are the cops who survive an entire career and earn their pension and then go riding off into the sunset.

Twenty five years on the street is a long time.

It's a lot of violent domestics, mind-numbing nightshifts, old people forgetting where they parked their cars, and dealing with problems within and without the system. It's a lot of holidays and birthdays with the kids that you don't get to spend. It's a lot of "Daddy loves you," over the phone.

Twenty five years is a lot of child victims.

A lot of bad, bad dreams.

It's a long time to wait for a pension that you might not live long enough to collect much from. A long time to go without getting in some sort of trouble off-duty that violated some rule or another, or to keep all the craziness you see pent up inside.

Most guys I've seen retire practically get a kick in the ass on the way out and a "Thanks for everything." You can almost hear the locks being changed the moment they leave the building.

You can see it in a retired guy's eyes.

A weariness with the world etched into their faces like crow's feet. All the instincts are still there. They'll still eye up a skell in the checkout line, give him a visual pat-down, maybe glance toward the door for the lookout man. They're like retired racehorses. They look at the track and everything inside them says, Run! They're too damned stubborn to realize they're obsolete.

A forty year veteran officer who is retired one day has less police authority than any rookie five seconds after taking the oath to Protect and Serve.

Fact.

And your time holding the True Blue Line will end as well, eventually. As will mine. Some guys can't let it go. It's too much a part of who they are, too deeply embedded in their personalities. They crave the authority and the respect that comes from being a police officer, just like some supervisors crave the ability to make people do what they say.

Remember that being a police officer is a job. It's a good job, and it's an important job, and it important you take it seriously, but it isn't your life. Find other things you enjoy and find fulfilling, continue to educate yourself about the world around you and cherish your loved ones.

If The Job has taught me one thing, it's that life is precious. All life is precious and must be protected, and that includes mine and yours outside of work.

I feel enormous gratitude toward the men and women I've worked with or known over the years. It takes a special breed of person to come running to a stranger's assistance, in risk of their own safety. It takes a true hero to do all those child sex victim interviews and crime scene investigations and years and years of rotating shifts.

I admire all of you and honor you as what you truly are: Warriors. Peace keepers. Answerers of the emergency call.

When the day comes that I leave, I know I will feel an enormous sense of relief and liberty. I also know that the day will come when I hear sirens going past my house and feel a longing to jump in.

Until then, I'll be out there just like you. Taking those calls. Rolling the dice. Doing what needs to be done. Because really, we only get a short amount of time to be among that elite warrior society who hold the True Blue Line. Many have come before, and many will come after, but for now, it's up to us and I am at your side, telling you to hang in there when you need it, hearing you say it when I need the same thing.

Always remember this.

You will face a multitude of challenges during the course of your career. Both personally and professionally. You will encounter seemingly never-ending complications and set-backs. That's okay. As long as you keep the faith and be true to yourself and your profession, no set-back will keep you down for very long. After all you were trained from the beginning to adapt. Improvise. Overcome.

Be safe.

Wear your vest. Buckle your seatbelt. Know your equipment. Tell the truth. Defend the innocent.

And no matter what, never surrender, and always get home.

8. A Word about this Edition

The two biggest complaints I get from readers about Way of the Warrior is that it's too short and there's no print edition. It shows up in the reviews, my emails, and my Facebook page. The original publication was around 12k words, little more than a long essay.

The latest email I received was from a narcotics sergeant in Maryland. He told me that his department is going through some serious changes and the guys are struggling. He asked me if there was a print version of this book he could pass around to help boost morale.

I've got to be honest, those emails really blow me away.

When I first set out to write Way of the Warrior, I was trying to document some of the good advice I've received and theories I've developed over the years. I never really expected anyone to pay attention. In many ways, when I read your emails and reviews, I look over both shoulders and look for the other guy you all must be talking about.

That being said, when a cop asks another cop for help, it's important to come through.

So, Sergeant Ryan Frashure and the hard-working men and women of Ann Arundel County, Maryland, I am pleased to dedicate this new edition to you. I will be sending you ten printed copies of the book as soon as it is available, and I hope you find some small part of it useful.

As I told Ryan in one of our emails, I was lucky enough to spend a week with Baltimore Homicide very early in my police career. Detective Dennis Raftery took me into his home and put up with all of my questions and gave me some of the same ideas you see me repeating here.

If this is one of the small ways I'm able to give back to that region, I'm extremely proud and honored to do so.

Bernard Schaffer
November 2013
Montgomery County, Pennsylvania

Bernard Schaffer is the author of multiple titles in a wide-variety of genres including: Superbia, a hard-hitting police procedural series about subversive cops trying to do right in a dirty world; Guns of Seneca 6, a six-part saga of the Old West in outer space; Grendel Unit, military science fiction about a team of operatives taking out terrorist threats to the galaxy.

His other work includes The Girl From Tenerife, a moving and honest account of falling in love with the wrong woman; Whitechapel: The Final Stand of Sherlock Holmes, a factual (and graphic) portrayal of Jack the Ripper's murders combined with the characters from Baker Street; and Tiny Dragons, a new children's fantasy series written specifically for his young daughter.

In addition to writing, Schaffer is the father of two children and a lifelong resident of the Philadelphia region. He spent his youth as a child actor and is now a decorated police veteran and expert witness in narcotics distribution.

Way of the Warrior

Bernard Schaffer

Published by Apiary Society Publications

Edited by Laurie Laliberte

Copyright 2013 Bernard Schaffer

All rights reserved. The following is a non-fiction essay based on the author's personal views and do not reflect any agency or other entity.

Made in the USA
Middletown, DE
14 January 2015